BREAKING INTO SAFETY

A Practical Career Guide For Men And Women Ready For The Field

By

Sharon Jost

TABLE OF CONTENTS

CHAPTER 1

IS SAFETY THE RIGHT CAREER FOR YOU?

A lot of people think safety is just about rules, paperwork, and telling others what they're doing wrong. That couldn't be further from the truth.

Safety is a people job first — and a technical job second.

Over the years, I've seen many people step into safety roles, thinking it's a comfortable position behind a clipboard. The reality is very different. You're working with crews, supervisors, and employees who are under pressure to get the job done. Your ability to communicate, build trust, and stay approachable matters just as much as your knowledge of standards and procedures.

Some people struggle in safety, not because they lack intelligence or training, but because they lack the interpersonal skills the role demands. If you can't talk to people respectfully, listen without judgment, or correct behavior without creating conflict, the job becomes harder than it needs to be.

A good safety professional isn't there to police workers — they're there to support them. The goal is to create an environment where people feel comfortable asking questions, reporting concerns, and working together to prevent incidents. That requires patience, emotional intelligence, and the ability to read situations before reacting.

Ask yourself honestly:

- Are you comfortable talking to people from all backgrounds?

- Can you give feedback without sounding confrontational?

- Do you stay calm when tensions rise?

- Are you willing to earn trust instead of demanding authority?

If the answer is yes, you're already building the foundation for a successful safety career.

This work isn't about being the loudest voice on the site. It's about being the steady presence people respect and rely on. When employees see you as approachable and fair, they listen. When they trust you, they involve you. And when that happens, safety becomes a shared effort — not a forced one.

Safety is a career that rewards professionalism, empathy, and strong communication. If you enjoy working with people, solving problems, and making environments safer, you'll find this field both challenging and deeply fulfilling.

And if you're willing to grow these skills along the way, you'll stand out in a profession where the human side of the job matters just as much as the technical side.

That's where real safety leadership begins.

The Myth of the "Easy" Safety Job

One of the biggest misconceptions about safety is that it's an easy position — a job where you carry a clipboard, walk around, and don't have to work as hard as everyone else.

That idea couldn't be more wrong.

Safety professionals are responsible for protecting people in environments where mistakes can lead to serious injuries, shutdowns, or worse. The pressure is real. You're constantly balancing productivity, compliance, communication, and human behavior — often all at the same time.

This isn't a role for someone looking to avoid effort. It's a role for someone willing to stay alert, engaged, and accountable throughout the entire workday. You're observing conditions, coaching employees, addressing concerns, documenting issues, and sometimes making difficult calls that impact schedules and operations.

The work can be mentally demanding. You're expected to notice details others overlook, speak up when something isn't right, and maintain professionalism even when conversations become uncomfortable.

People who enter safety thinking it's a shortcut to an easy paycheck usually discover quickly that the job requires presence, judgment, and strong communication skills. It's not about doing less — it's about doing work that carries weight and responsibility.

When done correctly, safety is one of the most meaningful roles on a jobsite. You're helping create an environment where people go home in the same condition they arrived — and that responsibility deserves commitment, not shortcuts.

If you're looking for a career where effort matters and your work makes a real difference, safety can be incredibly rewarding. But it's not easy — and it shouldn't be.

Safety Means Speaking Up — Often in Front of a Crowd

One part of safety that surprises many newcomers is how much public speaking the job requires.

Whether you're leading toolbox talks, conducting safety meetings, onboarding new workers, or addressing jobsite concerns, you will regularly find yourself speaking in front of groups. Sometimes it's a small crew. Other times it's dozens of people waiting for direction before work begins.

This isn't optional — it's a core responsibility.

Your ability to communicate clearly can influence how seriously safety is taken. When you speak with confidence, preparation, and professionalism, people listen. When your message is unclear or rushed, important information can be missed.

Public speaking in safety isn't about being a performer. It's about delivering information in a way that's understandable, practical, and respectful. You're guiding behavior, setting expectations, and reinforcing a culture where awareness matters.

Many successful safety professionals didn't start out comfortable speaking to groups. It's a skill that improves with practice. The key is preparation, knowing your material, and remembering that your goal is to help — not impress.

When crews see that you communicate clearly and consistently, trust grows. And in safety, trust is everything.

If the idea of speaking in front of others makes you nervous, don't let that stop you. Consider it a skill you'll develop along the way — one that will strengthen your credibility and effectiveness in the field.

CHAPTER 2

UNDERSTANDING THE PATH INTO SAFETY

So you've read what this career really demands — communication, professionalism, awareness, and the ability to work with people under pressure. And if you're still here thinking, "Yes — this is what I want," then the next question becomes:

Where do I start?

The good news is there isn't just one doorway into safety. People enter this field from many directions — construction trades, industrial work, military backgrounds, formal education programs, and career changes later in life. What matters most is not where you begin, but how intentionally you build your foundation.

Starting a safety career is about combining education, certifications, and real-world exposure. Each piece strengthens your credibility and prepares you for the responsibilities that come with protecting workers in active environments.

One of the biggest mistakes newcomers make is trying to rush the process. Safety isn't a title you earn overnight — it's a profession you grow into. Employers look for people who demonstrate commitment, willingness to learn, and respect for the role. Certifications help open doors, but mindset and preparation determine how far you go once you step inside.

In this chapter, we're going to break down the practical path forward:

- Education options and what employers actually value

- Entry-level certifications and how they fit into your career

- The difference between classroom knowledge and field readiness

- How to position yourself for your first opportunity

* Building experience while continuing to grow

Think of this as your roadmap — not a rigid checklist, but a clear guide to help you move forward with purpose. You don't need to know everything on day one. You need direction, discipline, and the willingness to keep building.

Safety is a career that rewards preparation. The more intentional you are about learning the field, the more confident you'll feel stepping into your first role.

Let's start with education — and what actually matters when employers are deciding who to hire.

Education Path Example: Building a Foundation Through a Safety Degree

One strong way to enter the safety field is through a structured education program. While there are multiple routes into this profession, a degree focused on occupational safety provides a solid foundation in hazard recognition, compliance, risk management, and professional communication.

For example, Columbia Southern University offers accredited safety programs designed specifically for working adults and career changers. Their programs include specialized tracks such as construction safety, oil and gas safety, and maritime safety — allowing students to focus on the environments they want to work in. Because coursework is delivered online, it gives students flexibility to balance education with work and personal responsibilities.

Pursuing an associate or bachelor's degree in safety demonstrates commitment to the profession and provides knowledge that translates directly into the field. Employers value candidates who understand both regulatory standards and practical application.

Graduates of qualifying bachelor's safety programs may also earn a Graduate Safety Practitioner (GSP) designation through the Board of Certified Safety Professionals. The GSP is recognized as a pathway toward advanced certifications and signals that the individual has completed an accredited safety curriculum.

Education alone does not make someone an effective safety professional — but it builds the framework needed to grow. Combined with field experience, strong communication skills, and continued learning, a structured program can significantly accelerate your entry into the profession.

The key is choosing an education path that aligns with your goals, schedule, and long-term vision in safety.

Competition in the Safety Field — Why Preparation Matters

The safety profession has grown significantly over the years. More people are recognizing it as a meaningful and stable career path — which also means competition has increased.

Today, employers often have multiple qualified candidates applying for the same role. While experience and communication skills remain critical, formal education and recognized certifications can make a major difference when hiring decisions are made.

Having a degree in safety or a closely related field demonstrates commitment and foundational knowledge. Pairing that education with certifications recognized by the Board of Certified Safety Professionals (BCSP) signals that you take professional development seriously. Together, these credentials help position you as someone who is invested in the career — not just exploring it casually.

This doesn't mean success is limited to those with degrees alone. Many strong safety professionals come from trade backgrounds or hands-on experience. However, in a competitive environment, combining real-world understanding with formal credentials gives you an advantage and opens doors faster.

Think of education and certification as tools that strengthen your credibility. They don't replace professionalism, communication, or work ethic — but they reinforce them. When employers see preparation, they see someone ready to grow within the role.

In a field where responsibility is high and expectations are evolving, investing in your qualifications is one of the smartest steps you can take toward long-term success.

The Mistake of Chasing Titles Too Fast

One of the most common traps new safety professionals fall into is chasing certifications and titles before they've built the experience to support them.

Ambition is healthy — but safety certifications are not easy exams. They're designed to measure real understanding, judgment, and practical application. When someone rushes into testing without enough hands-on exposure, the material can feel overwhelming, and failed attempts become more likely.

These exams aren't meant to be shortcuts. They validate knowledge that grows through real-world experience — observing hazards, communicating with crews, and making decisions in active environments. Without that foundation, studying turns into memorization instead of comprehension.

Passing a certification exam requires preparation, field awareness, and patience. Titles alone don't create credibility — experience does. Workers and supervisors respect professionals who demonstrate calm decision-making and practical understanding, not just letters behind their name.

The strongest safety professionals focus on steady progression. They build their skills in the field, study with intention, and pursue certification when they're truly ready. When you respect the process, certification becomes proof of growth — not just a milestone.

Safety is a profession where preparation matters. Take the time to build the foundation first. The titles will come — and when they do, they'll mean something.

What OSHA Credential Tracks Typically Involve: CSHO and SHEP

Understanding what OSHA-based credentials require helps you plan your training realistically. These programs are built around structured coursework that emphasizes hazard recognition, compliance knowledge, and real-world safety application.

The Certified Safety and Health Official (CSHO) credential is earned by completing a core sequence of OSHA training courses along with several elective classes. Foundational coursework commonly includes OSHA standards training covering both construction and general industry environments. Candidates then complete additional OSHA-approved classes that focus on practical safety topics such as electrical standards, industrial hygiene, scaffolding, fall protection, or similar hazard-specific areas.

The goal of the CSHO track is to develop broad, applied knowledge that prepares safety professionals to recognize risks and communicate standards effectively in the field. The coursework is designed to build confidence and reinforce compliance awareness across multiple environments.

The Safety, Health, and Environmental Professional (SHEP) credential builds on the CSHO foundation. After completing the required OSHA coursework, candidates expand their training into environmental awareness, risk management principles, and air or exposure-related safety topics. This added focus reflects a more comprehensive understanding of workplace safety that includes environmental and operational risk considerations.

While exact course requirements and availability may evolve over time, these credential tracks consistently emphasize practical learning and continuing professional development. They are structured to strengthen field readiness, reinforce standards knowledge, and support long-term career growth.

Candidates should always verify current course requirements through authorized OSHA training providers, as program structures and offerings can change. Planning ahead ensures your training aligns with your professional goals.

Understanding Major Safety Certifications and Career Pathways

Certifications are one of the strongest ways to demonstrate commitment and credibility in the safety profession. They signal to employers that you've invested time in learning standards, best practices, and professional responsibility. However, not all certifications serve the same purpose, and understanding the pathways can help you plan your career intentionally.

BCSP Certifications: Structured Professional Pathways

The Board of Certified Safety Professionals (BCSP) offers nationally recognized credentials that many employers view as industry benchmarks. These certifications are tied to specific education and experience requirements, which means they reflect both knowledge and time spent working in the field.

Entry and mid level certifications, such as the Construction Health and Safety Technician (CHST), are designed for professionals actively working in construction environments. Eligibility generally requires documented safety experience and employer verification of duties related to hazard recognition and prevention.

Advanced credentials, like the Certified Safety Professional (CSP), represent a higher professional tier. Candidates typically need a qualifying degree or recognized pathway credential, along with several years of professional safety experience. The CSP exam evaluates technical knowledge, decision-making, and practical application — making it one of the most respected certifications in the field.

BCSP certifications emphasize progression. As your experience grows, you move toward higher credentials that reflect deeper expertise and leadership capability.

OSHA-Based Certifications: Practical Field Credentials

OSHA-related certifications, such as the Certified Safety and Health Official (CSHO) and the Safety, Health, and Environmental Professional (SHEP), focus heavily on applied training. These programs involve completing structured OSHA coursework covering hazard recognition, compliance principles, and industry-specific safety topics.

Rather than being tied strictly to degree requirements, OSHA-based credentials emphasize continuing education and hands-on learning. Many employers — especially in construction-heavy environments — recognize these certifications as strong indicators of practical knowledge.

Some organizations view advanced OSHA credential tracks as comparable to formal education when evaluating candidates, particularly when paired with field experience. The value comes from demonstrated training and ongoing professional development.

Regional Perspectives and Employer Expectations

How certifications are valued can vary depending on geographic region and industry culture. In some areas, employers prioritize

BCSP credentials and may use them as a benchmark for advancement into higher-level safety roles.

In other regions, OSHA-based certifications carry strong recognition, especially in industries where practical training and compliance familiarity are highly emphasized. Neither path is inherently superior — they simply represent different approaches to building professional credibility.

The most competitive safety professionals often combine both structured certifications and practical coursework. This balanced approach signals adaptability, dedication, and a commitment to continuous learning.

Ultimately, certifications are tools — they strengthen your resume, expand your knowledge, and help employers understand your preparation. Choosing the right pathway depends on your career goals, experience level, and the environment you plan to work in.

Practical Certification Snapshot: Experience, Costs, and Expectations

Understanding the general requirements and costs associated with safety certifications helps you plan your professional timeline with confidence. While exact criteria may change over time, the following overview reflects the typical structure candidates encounter.

For example, the Construction Health and Safety Technician (CHST) certification is designed for professionals actively working in construction environments. Eligibility commonly includes approximately three years of verified experience in a role where a significant portion of job duties — often around one-third or more — involve safety responsibilities such as hazard recognition and prevention.

The application process typically includes an initial review fee. Once approved, candidates are given a defined window to schedule and complete the exam. After certification is earned, annual renewal fees support credential maintenance and continuing professional standards.

Advanced certifications follow a progression model. The Certified Safety Professional (CSP) credential is considered a higher-level designation requiring documented professional safety experience and prerequisite qualifications. Many candidates first earn an associate-level certification that validates their foundational knowledge before advancing toward the CSP.

Graduates of qualifying safety degree programs may earn a Graduate Safety Practitioner (GSP) designation, which can streamline progression by satisfying certain prerequisite requirements. This pathway reflects the value of accredited education combined with real-world experience.

Because certification costs, eligibility percentages, and experience documentation standards evolve, candidates should always verify current requirements directly through the certifying organization before applying.

The takeaway is simple: certification is not just an exam — it's a structured professional journey. Planning ahead allows you to align your education, experience, and financial investment in a way that supports long-term growth in the safety field.

CHAPTER 3
LANDING YOUR FIRST SAFETY JOB

Once you've started building your education, certifications, and understanding of the safety profession, the next step is turning preparation into opportunity. Landing your first safety job is where planning meets reality — and knowing what to expect gives you a major advantage.

One of the best places to begin your search is through professional job platforms such as LinkedIn and Indeed. These sites allow you to see what employers are looking for, compare qualifications, and identify entry-level opportunities that align with your current experience. Even if you don't meet every listed requirement, applying strategically and presenting yourself professionally can open doors.

It's important to approach your first safety role with realistic expectations. Many newcomers make the mistake of assuming certifications or coursework automatically translate into top-tier pay. In reality, safety is a profession where credibility is built through time, field exposure, and demonstrated reliability.

Your first position is about learning — observing how experienced professionals communicate, how sites operate, and how safety programs function in real environments. Compensation grows alongside your skill set, certifications, and ability to contribute meaningfully to operations.

Starting at an entry level isn't a setback — it's a foundation. Every safety professional who advances in this field has spent time building experience, earning trust, and strengthening their credentials. As certifications accumulate and field confidence increases, your value — and earning potential — naturally rise.

Approach your first job with humility, professionalism, and a willingness to grow. Employers notice candidates who show initiative, adaptability, and respect for the learning process. That mindset creates opportunities far faster than chasing titles or pay alone.

Landing your first safety role isn't the finish line — it's the starting point of a career built on continuous development. When you focus on learning first, advancement follows.

What Employers Are Really Looking For — And What Safety Work Looks Like in the Field

When employers hire a safety professional — especially someone entering the field — they're not just looking for certifications or coursework. They're looking for someone who can operate confidently around people, communicate clearly, and support safe work in real-time environments.

Safety in the field is active work. It's not a desk position where you simply review paperwork. A large part of the role involves being present on the jobsite, observing tasks, and identifying conditions that could lead to injury or incident.

Daily responsibilities often include conducting job-site observations and high-risk activity assessments. These evaluations help crews recognize hazards before work begins and encourage thoughtful planning. Safety professionals may also assist employees with pre-task planning boards, helping them walk through the steps of a job, identify risks, and establish protective measures.

Equally important is coaching. Safety isn't about catching people doing something wrong — it's about guiding them toward safer choices. That requires patience, approachability, and the ability to communicate without creating defensiveness. Workers respond best when they feel supported rather than judged.

Employers value safety professionals who are personable, calm
under pressure, and willing to engage with crews respectfully. The
ability to build trust makes observations more effective and
conversations more productive.

At its core, field safety work is about presence and partnership.
You're helping teams think ahead, reduce risk, and maintain
awareness — not by authority alone, but by communication and
consistency.

When employers see candidates who understand this human side
of safety, they see someone ready to grow into the role. Technical
knowledge matters, but the ability to work with people is what turns
knowledge into real world impact.

Building Trust with Crews

Trust is the foundation of effective safety work. Without it,
conversations feel forced, observations are ignored, and safety
becomes something workers tolerate instead of support.

Crews can quickly sense whether a safety professional is there to
help or simply enforce rules. The difference comes down to how you
show up every day.

Building trust starts with respect. Speak to workers as
professionals who understand their trade, not as people waiting to be
corrected. Ask questions before giving direction. Listen to their
perspective. When employees feel heard, they are far more willing to
engage in safety discussions.

Consistency matters just as much as attitude. If you enforce
standards one day and overlook them the next, credibility disappears.
Fairness builds confidence. Workers need to know your expectations
are steady and that your decisions are grounded in safety — not
personal preference.

Visibility is another key factor. Being present in the field shows that you're invested in the work environment, not hiding behind paperwork. When crews see you regularly observing tasks, offering guidance, and checking in, safety becomes part of the workflow instead of an interruption.

Trust also grows when you admit what you don't know. No safety professional has every answer. Being willing to research a concern or ask for clarification demonstrates honesty and professionalism — qualities crew's respect.

Above all, remember that trust is built through partnership. Safety is most effective when workers view you as an ally working toward the same goal: everyone going home safe at the end of the day.

When trust is established, communication improves, hazards are reported sooner, and cooperation becomes natural. That's when safety moves beyond compliance and becomes culture.

CHAPTER 4

THE REALITY OF CONSTRUCTION SAFETY LIFE

Construction safety can be an incredibly rewarding career — but it comes with a lifestyle that many people don't fully understand until they're living it.

Long hours are common. Sixty-hour workweeks are not unusual in active construction environments, especially on large projects or tight schedules. The pace can be demanding, and over time, those hours take a physical and mental toll. Staying alert, present, and professional throughout extended shifts requires discipline and resilience.

For many safety professionals, travel is part of the job. Living out of a suitcase becomes normal. Hotels and short-term rentals replace the comfort of home, and meals often come from restaurants or quick stops between shifts because there simply isn't time to cook. Maintaining healthy habits takes intention when your routine constantly changes.

Time away from home is one of the hardest realities of the field. Missing family events, holidays, or everyday moments can weigh heavily, especially on long projects. Construction safety is not just a job — it's a lifestyle commitment that affects both you and the people who support you.

At the same time, this career can offer strong financial rewards. Travel assignments and demanding schedules are often matched by competitive pay and opportunities for advancement. Many professionals view this balance as a tradeoff — hard work and sacrifice in exchange for meaningful income and career growth.

The key is understanding what you're signing up for. Construction safety isn't a nine-to-five desk role. It's a field-driven profession that requires adaptability, endurance, and personal discipline. When approached with realistic expectations and strong boundaries, it can be both sustainable and fulfilling.

Knowing the lifestyle ahead of time allows you to plan — financially, physically, and emotionally — so you can thrive instead of simply endure.

Managing Burnout, Staying Healthy on the Road, and Finding Balance

Construction safety work demands long hours, constant focus, and extended time away from home. Over time, that pace can wear down even the most dedicated professionals if intentional habits aren't built to support physical and mental health.

Burnout doesn't happen overnight. It builds quietly — fatigue, irritability, reduced motivation, and the feeling that work never truly stops. Many safety professionals push through these warning signs because the job requires presence and accountability. But ignoring burnout only makes recovery harder.

Travel assignments add another layer of challenge. Living in hotels or short-term housing often means inconsistent routines and limited access to home-cooked meals. Fast food becomes convenient, sleep schedules shift, and exercise gets pushed aside. Without awareness, these patterns can quickly affect energy, focus, and long-term health.

Protecting your well-being starts with intention. Prioritize sleep whenever possible. Choose healthier food options when traveling. Build simple movement into your day — even short walks or bodyweight exercises help counter long shifts. Small habits practiced consistently have a compounding effect.

Equally important is emotional balance. Construction safety can become all-consuming, especially during critical project phases. Setting boundaries — even small ones — helps preserve your energy. Schedule regular check-ins with family, maintain hobbies when possible, and give yourself permission to disconnect after work hours.

Work-life balance in this field rarely looks perfect. There will be seasons where work dominates your schedule. The goal isn't perfection — it's sustainability. Money and advancement are meaningful, but they lose value if your health or relationships suffer.

The strongest safety professionals recognize that longevity matters. Taking care of your body, your mindset, and your personal life allows you to continue performing at a high level without sacrificing yourself in the process.

This career is demanding — but with awareness and discipline, it can be navigated in a way that supports both professional success and personal well-being.

Knowing When to Step Back

Construction safety professionals are often wired to push forward. The job demands focus, responsibility, and long hours — and many people pride themselves on being the one who can handle the pressure. But part of long-term success in this field is recognizing when stepping back is not weakness, but wisdom.

There are times when fatigue, stress, or personal circumstances begin to affect your ability to perform at your best. Safety work requires clear thinking and strong judgment. When exhaustion or burnout clouds that judgment, the risks extend beyond personal discomfort — they impact the environment and people around you.

Stepping back doesn't always mean leaving a job or walking away from the profession. Sometimes it means requesting time off, rotating assignments, adjusting schedules, or having honest conversations with leadership about workload. Other times it means reassessing priorities to protect your health or relationships.

The safety profession is built on prevention — identifying hazards before they become incidents. That mindset applies to your own well-being as well. Recognizing early signs of strain and addressing them proactively is part of being a responsible professional.

A sustainable career is not measured by how much you can endure without rest. It's measured by your ability to maintain clarity, professionalism, and effectiveness over time. Protecting your energy ensures you can continue doing meaningful work without sacrificing your health or personal life.

Knowing when to step back is not stepping away from commitment — it's reinforcing it. When you care for yourself, you strengthen your ability to care for others and remain a steady presence in a demanding profession.

CHAPTER 5

BECOMING A RESPECTED SAFETY PROFESSIONAL — AND THE MISTAKES THAT CAN HURT YOUR CAREER

A successful safety career is built on more than certifications and job titles. It's built on credibility — the trust you earn from crews, supervisors, and leadership through your actions, communication, and consistency.

Respect in the field isn't automatic. It grows over time as people observe how you handle pressure, how you speak to others, and how committed you are to doing the job the right way. The professionals who stand out are those who combine technical knowledge with strong people skills and steady judgment.

One of the fastest ways to build respect is through professionalism. Show up prepared, communicate clearly, and follow through on what you say. Workers quickly notice who is reliable and who isn't. Consistency builds confidence — and confidence builds credibility.

Equally important is approachability. Safety is a partnership, not a power position. When employees feel comfortable bringing concerns to you, hazards are addressed sooner, and trust deepens. Listening is just as important as speaking.

However, credibility can be damaged just as quickly as it's built.

A common mistake is leading with authority instead of understanding. Correcting everything immediately without learning the work environment creates resistance. Respect grows when guidance is delivered thoughtfully and with context.

Another career-limiting mistake is chasing titles without building real experience. Certifications should support field knowledge, not replace it. When advancement outpaces understanding, confidence suffers, and credibility weakens.

Communication missteps can also hurt long-term reputation. Speaking harshly, dismissing concerns, or escalating minor issues unnecessarily erodes trust. Safety professionals are most effective when their tone remains calm, respectful, and solution-focused.

Finally, ignoring personal well-being leads to burnout — and burnout affects judgment, patience, and performance. A respected professional knows when to slow down, ask for support, and protect their ability to perform consistently.

The path to becoming a trusted safety professional is not about perfection. It's about intention — choosing behaviors that build credibility while avoiding habits that undermine it. When professionalism, humility, and growth remain priorities, respect follows naturally.

And in safety, respect is one of your most powerful tools.

CHAPTER 6

GROWING BEYOND THE BASICS — FROM SAFETY REPRESENTATIVE TO SAFETY LEADER

There comes a point in every safety career where the role begins to shift.

Early on, your focus is learning the job — understanding hazards, applying standards, building trust, and finding your footing in the field. But as experience grows, expectations change. You're no longer just expected to identify problems. You're expected to help solve them.

This is where the transition from safety representative to safety leader begins.

Safety leadership is not defined by title. It's defined by influence. Leaders are the professionals' others look to when conditions are uncertain, decisions are difficult, or pressure is high. They don't just point out what's wrong — they help chart a path forward.

The Shift from Observation to Influence

In the early stages of your career, much of your work revolves around observation: identifying hazards, documenting issues, and ensuring compliance.

As you grow, your role becomes more strategic.

You begin asking deeper questions:

- Why does this issue keep recurring?

- What systems are contributing to this behavior?

- How can safety be integrated earlier into planning instead of reacting afterward?

Leadership in safety means thinking beyond individual acts and looking at patterns, processes, and culture. It means working with supervisors and management to address root causes — not just symptoms.

When safety becomes proactive instead of reactive, real change happens.

Learning to Work with Leadership — Not Against It

One of the biggest adjustments in advancing your career is learning how to work effectively with management.

Leadership teams are balancing budgets, schedules, manpower, and client expectations. Safety leaders understand these pressures and communicate in a way that aligns protection with productivity — not opposition.

This doesn't mean compromising safety. It means framing safety as a solution, not an obstacle.

When you can explain how a safety improvement prevents delays, reduces injuries, protects morale, and saves money, leadership listens. The language you use matters. Clear, professional communication builds credibility at higher levels just as it does in the field.

Safety leaders learn to speak both languages — the language of the workforce and the language of management.

Taking Ownership of Programs and Outcomes

As responsibility increases, so does ownership.

Safety leaders are often responsible for developing or improving programs — orientations, training, audits, or site-specific plans. This requires organization, follow-through, and accountability.

Owning a program means more than creating paperwork. It means ensuring the process actually works in real conditions. Effective leaders seek feedback, adjust when needed, and continuously improve.

Mistakes will happen. What matters is how they're handled. Taking responsibility, correcting issues, and learning from outcomes strengthens trust and demonstrates maturity.

Leadership is built through accountability, not perfection.

Mentoring Others — A Sign You've Grown

One of the clearest signs that you're progressing in your career is when others begin coming to you for guidance.

Mentoring newer safety professionals or workers isn't about showing superiority — it's about sharing knowledge responsibly. Teaching reinforces your own understanding and strengthens the overall safety culture.

Strong leaders remember what it was like to be new. They correct without discouraging. They guide without belittling. And they invest in others because they understand that safety is a shared responsibility.

Your influence multiplies when you help others grow.

Choosing Your Direction Intentionally

As your experience expands, so do your options.

Some safety professionals choose to specialize — construction, oil and gas, industrial hygiene, environmental safety, or auditing.

Others move toward management, consulting, or corporate leadership roles.

There is no single "right" path. The key is intentionality.

Ask yourself:

- Do I enjoy field work or strategic planning more?

- Do I prefer travel or stability?

- Do I want to lead teams, advise organizations, or specialize technically?

Your answers will guide your next certifications, roles, and opportunities. Growth without direction can lead to frustration. Growth with intention builds fulfillment.

Leadership Is a Responsibility — Not a Reward

Advancing in safety is not about status. It's about responsibility.

As influence grows, so does impact — on workers, operations, and outcomes. The decisions you help shape can affect livelihoods, health, and lives. That weight requires humility, preparation, and integrity.

The most effective safety leaders never forget why the role exists: to protect people.

When leadership is grounded in that purpose, careers become meaningful — not just successful.

CHAPTER 7

THE LONG-TERM CONSULTING PATH — BUILDING INDEPENDENCE, AUTHORITY, AND SUSTAINABILITY

For many safety professionals, consulting becomes the long-term goal — not because it's easier, but because it offers autonomy, influence, and control over how your expertise is used.

Consulting is not an entry-level move. It's the result of years spent building credibility in the field, learning how organizations operate, and understanding how safety decisions impact production, budgets, and people. When done correctly, consulting allows you to leverage experience rather than trade time for constant supervision.

This chapter focuses on what the consulting path really looks like — beyond the title.

Why Experienced Safety Professionals Move into Consulting

Consulting appeals to professionals who have already proven themselves in the field and leadership roles. By the time someone transitions into consulting, they usually have:

- Strong field credibility

- The ability to communicate with both crews and executives

- Confidence making independent decisions

- A deep understanding of compliance and operations

Many reach a point where they want more control over projects, schedules, and income. Consulting allows experienced professionals to provide value without being tied to one company's internal politics or limitations.

It's a shift from being managed — to being trusted.

Consulting Is a Business, Not Just a Skillset

One of the biggest misconceptions about consulting is thinking it's simply "doing safety work independently."

In reality, consulting is a business.

Technical knowledge alone is not enough. Long-term consultants understand contracts, scope of work, invoicing, insurance, and client expectations. They protect their reputation and their time as carefully as they protect workers.

Sustainable consultants know how to:

- Define clear deliverables

- Price their expertise appropriately

- Avoid scope creep

- Document decisions and recommendations

- Maintain professional boundaries

Consulting rewards professionals who are organized, disciplined, and confident in their value.

Building Authority Instead of Chasing Clients

Successful consultants don't beg for work. They build authority.

Authority comes from consistency — showing up prepared, communicating clearly, and delivering what was promised. Over time, referrals replace cold outreach. Clients return because trust has already been established.

The strongest consultants:

- Solve problems, not just identify them

- Speak in solutions leadership understands

- Stay calm under pressure

- Know when to push and when to advise

Your name becomes your brand. That reputation is what sustains consulting long term.

Choosing the Right Consulting Model

Not all consulting looks the same. Long term success depends on choosing a model that fits your lifestyle and goals.

Some consultants remain field-heavy, supporting large projects on a contract basis. Others focus on audits, program development, or compliance support. Some transition into advisory roles working directly with executives.

Each model has tradeoffs:

- Field consulting offers higher day rates but heavier schedules

- Advisory consulting offers flexibility but requires deeper trust

- Project-based work provides structure but limits availability

The most sustainable careers often blend multiple approaches over time.

Income Reality — Consulting Rewards Experience

Consulting can be financially rewarding, but it's not instant.

Income grows as your reputation grows. Early consulting may feel inconsistent. Long-term consulting becomes stable when relationships and referrals are established.

Experienced consultants command higher rates because they reduce risk. Clients pay for judgment, not just presence. They pay because your advice prevents shutdowns, injuries, and liability.

When consulting is done well, income reflects expertise — not hours logged.

Avoiding Burnout as a Consultant

Independence comes with responsibility.

Without boundaries, consulting can become just as exhausting as field work — sometimes more. Long-term consultants learn to say no, choose clients carefully, and protect their energy.

Sustainability requires:

- Clear contracts

- Defined availability

- Strategic project selection

- Periodic downtime

Consulting should provide freedom — not recreate burnout under a different title.

Consulting as a Legacy Career

The most successful consultants don't just work — they advise, mentor, and shape systems.

Over time, many transition into:

* Training and mentorship

* Program design and audits

* Strategic advisory roles

* Thought leadership and writing

Consulting becomes less about being everywhere — and more about being trusted.

That's the long-term power of the consulting path.

Consulting Is Earned, Not Given

Consulting is not a shortcut. It's a culmination.

It rewards professionals who respected the process, built credibility, and learned how to lead without authority. Those who reach this stage understand that influence is more powerful than position.

When done intentionally, consulting becomes more than a career move — it becomes a sustainable, independent, and deeply fulfilling way to apply everything you've learned.

Chapter 8

Entering the Consulting World — What Changes and What Doesn't

Moving into consulting is not about abandoning safety fundamentals — it's about applying them differently.

At its core, the work remains the same: protecting people, reducing risk, and helping organizations operate safely. What changes is how you deliver that value and how you are perceived.

When you step into consulting, you are no longer "part of the team" by default. You are brought in because of what you know, how you think, and the judgment you provide. Your presence has purpose — and expectations are higher from day one.

The Shift from Employee to Advisor

As an employee, you operate within a company's structure. You follow internal processes, report through a chain of command, and focus on day-to-day execution.

As a consultant, your role is advisory.

You are expected to assess situations quickly, communicate clearly, and offer recommendations that leadership can act on. You are not there to manage personalities or navigate internal politics — you are there to provide clarity.

That shift requires confidence and restraint. Consultants must know when to speak, when to listen, and how to deliver uncomfortable truths professionally.

Your credibility is assumed — but it must be reinforced through competence and communication.

Consulting Requires Faster Judgment

In consulting, there is less ramp up time.

Clients expect you to recognize hazards, understand systems, and ask the right questions almost immediately. You are often stepping into environments with existing problems, tight timelines, or regulatory pressure.

This is why consulting is not entry-level work.

Strong consultants rely on experience, pattern recognition, and sound judgment. They don't panic under pressure, and they don't overreact. They evaluate conditions, identify priorities, and focus on what truly matters.

Calm, confident decision-making is one of the most valuable skills a consultant can offer.

Communication Becomes Even More Critical

In consulting, how you communicate can determine whether your recommendations are followed or ignored.

You must be able to:

- Explain risks clearly without alarming leadership

- Offer solutions that are practical, not theoretical

- Document findings professionally

- Speak with authority without arrogance

Consultants often deliver messages that internal staff cannot. That requires tact, clarity, and professionalism. Emotional intelligence becomes just as important as technical knowledge.

When clients trust your communication, they trust your judgment.

You Are Your Reputation

In consulting, there is no buffer.

Your name, behavior, and results follow you. Each project contributes to your professional reputation — positively or negatively. Word travels fast, especially in construction and industrial environments.

Being reliable matters. Meeting deadlines matters. Following through matters.

Consultants who overpromise, exaggerate expertise, or blur professional boundaries damage trust quickly — and that trust is difficult to regain.

The strongest consultants are consistent, measured, and honest about what they can and cannot deliver.

Consulting Does Not Mean Doing Everything

One of the hardest lessons new consultants learn is that saying yes to everything leads to poor outcomes.

Effective consultants define their role clearly. They understand the difference between advising and owning execution. They document recommendations and allow clients to decide how to proceed.

This protects both the consultant and the client.

Consulting is about guidance, not control. Knowing where your responsibility begins and ends is critical for professional integrity.

Why Some Safety Professionals Thrive in Consulting — and Others Don't

Consulting rewards a specific mindset.

Those who thrive are:

* Self-directed

* Comfortable with accountability

* Confident in their experience

* Professional under pressure

* Clear communicators

Those who struggle often expect the structure and protection of employment to remain. Consulting removes that structure — and replaces it with independence.

Understanding this difference before making the move prevents frustration and disappointment.

Consulting Is a Transition, not a Leap

Entering consulting doesn't require abandoning everything at once.

Many professionals begin by consulting on projects, supporting audits, or taking short-term assignments. These experiences build confidence and help clarify whether consulting truly fits their personality and goals.

The smartest transitions are intentional — not reactive.

Consulting works best when it's entered with preparation, self-awareness, and respect for the responsibility it carries.

CHAPTER 9

EARLY CONSULTING MISTAKES — AND HOW TO AVOID THEM

Many safety professionals enter consulting with strong technical skills and solid field experience — yet still struggle in the early stages. The reason is simple: consulting exposes gaps that traditional roles often protect you from.

This chapter isn't about discouragement. It's about awareness. Understanding common early mistakes allows you to avoid costly lessons and build credibility faster.

Mistake #1: Saying Yes to Everything

One of the most common early consulting mistakes is accepting every opportunity that comes along.

In the beginning, it feels smart. You want experience, income, and momentum. But saying yes without boundaries quickly leads to exhaustion, diluted focus, and underperformance.

Not every project is a good fit. Some clients lack clarity. Others expect unlimited availability or blurred responsibility. Accepting poorly defined work puts your reputation at risk.

How to avoid it:

Define your scope clearly before accepting work. Ask questions about expectations, deliverables, timelines, and authority. If something feels vague or unrealistic, pause. Protecting your standards protects your reputation.

Mistake #2: Undervaluing Your Expertise

Many new consultants struggle to price their services confidently.

After years as an employee, it can feel uncomfortable charging for judgment instead of hours worked. This often leads to underpricing, over-delivering, and resentment.

Clients do not pay consultants for presence — they pay for clarity, risk reduction, and informed decision-making.

How to avoid it:

Price based on value, not insecurity. Remember that your experience helps clients avoid incidents, fines, delays, and legal exposure. Confidence in your pricing communicates confidence in your expertise.

Mistake #3: Failing to Document Recommendations

Verbal guidance without documentation is a liability.

Early consultants sometimes rely too heavily on conversations, assuming their advice will be remembered or acted upon. When recommendations aren't documented, accountability becomes unclear — and risk shifts back to you.

How to avoid it:

Put recommendations in writing. Be clear, professional, and factual. Documentation protects both you and the client. It also reinforces your role as an advisor, not an enforcer.

Mistake #4: Acting Like an Employee Instead of a Consultant

Consultants who fall back into employee habits often struggle.

Over-involving themselves in daily operations, taking on tasks outside their scope, or managing people directly blurs boundaries and creates confusion. It can also expose you to unnecessary liability.

How to avoid it:

Stay in your lane. Advise, assess, recommend, and support — but don't assume ownership of execution unless it's explicitly part of the contract. Clarity maintains professionalism.

Mistake #5: Delivering the Message Poorly

Even accurate advice can fail if delivered poorly.

Being too blunt, overly technical, or dismissive of operational realities can cause leadership to disengage. Consulting requires diplomacy — not dilution of safety, but effective communication.

How to avoid it:

Frame recommendations in terms of solutions and outcomes. Explain risks calmly and professionally. Tailor your communication to your audience without compromising the message.

Mistake #6: Ignoring Legal and Business Basics

Some early consultants focus solely on safety and overlook the business side entirely.

Operating without contracts, insurance, or defined terms exposes you to significant risk. Professional independence requires professional structure.

How to avoid it:

Use written agreements. Maintain appropriate insurance. Clarify payment terms. Treat consulting like the business it is — not a side favor.

Mistake #7: Taking Resistance Personally

Resistance is part of consulting.

Clients may push back, delay action, or choose not to follow recommendations. New consultants sometimes internalize this as failure or respond emotionally.

How to avoid it:

Understand that your role is to advise, not control. Provide clear guidance, document recommendations, and allow clients to make informed decisions. Professional detachment preserves credibility.

Mistake #8: Burning Yourself Out Early

Independence often leads to overwork.

Without boundaries, consultants can quickly recreate the same burnout they hoped to escape — just without support or structure.

How to avoid it:

Set realistic availability. Build recovery time into your schedule. Sustainable consulting requires energy, focus, and clarity — not constant urgency.

Learning Faster Means Lasting Longer

Mistakes don't define a consulting career — how you respond to them does.

The most successful consultants learn quickly, adjust intentionally, and protect their professionalism. They understand that credibility is built through consistency, not perfection.

Early awareness shortens the learning curve. And a shorter learning curve builds confidence, stability, and respect.

CHAPTER 10

THE BUSINESS SIDE OF SAFETY — MASTERING 1099 INCOME, WRITE-OFFS, AND SMART TAX STRATEGY

Once you step into consulting, safety stops being just a profession — it becomes a business.

Many experienced safety professionals are technically excellent but financially unprepared for what 1099 income truly means. Without structure, strong income can turn into unnecessary tax exposure, cash-flow stress, and costly mistakes.

This chapter is about learning to think like a business owner — not just a consultant.

Understanding 1099 Income: Freedom with Responsibility

1099 income offers flexibility and control, but it also removes the protections built into traditional employment. There is no automatic tax withholding, no employer-paid benefits, and no safety net unless you create one.

Every dollar you earn is yours — but you are also responsible for:

- Federal income tax

- Self-employment tax

- State and local taxes (if applicable)

- Insurance and benefits

- Retirement planning

The consultants who succeed long term are not the ones who earn the most — they're the ones who manage cash intentionally.

Write-Offs Are a Strategy, not a Game

Deductions are not about "writing off everything." They are about accurately capturing the real cost of operating your business.

The guiding rule is simple:

If it is ordinary and necessary to produce income, it is likely deductible.

That includes:

- Travel required for work

- Vehicles used for business

- Technology and tools

- Education and certifications

- Professional insurance

- Marketing and client acquisition

Strong deductions reduce taxable income while keeping your business defensible. Sloppy deductions create audit risk and stress.

Travel and Vehicles: The Largest Deduction Categories

For many safety consultants, travel is unavoidable — and deductible.

Business travel expenses include airfare, lodging, rental cars, tolls, parking, and baggage fees when travel requires overnight stays. Meals while traveling are generally deductible at 50%.

Vehicle deductions require careful tracking. You may choose either the standard mileage method or actual expenses, but accuracy is critical. Mileage logs must be consistent and detailed.

This category alone can significantly reduce taxable income when managed correctly.

The Home Office: Powerful When Done Right

A legitimate home office can be one of the most valuable deductions — and one of the most misunderstood.

To qualify, the space must be used regularly and exclusively for business. When properly documented, a percentage of rent or mortgage interest, utilities, insurance, and repairs become deductible.

The key is reasonableness. Conservative calculations paired with strong documentation make this deduction both powerful and defensible.

Technology, Tools, and Professional Expenses

Consulting requires infrastructure. Phones, computers, software, cloud storage, and professional tools are not luxuries — they are business necessities.

These expenses are typically fully deductible or depreciated depending on size and usage. Subscription services that support scheduling, accounting, communication, or reporting are also legitimate deductions.

Education deserves special attention. Certifications, continuing education, exam fees, and industry conferences are clean, defensible write-offs when they enhance your current profession.

Insurance and Protection: Non-Negotiable Expenses

Professional independence increases liability.

General liability insurance, professional liability (errors and omissions), and business umbrella policies are fully deductible — and essential. These costs protect your income, your reputation, and your future.

Consultants who skip insurance to save money often pay far more later.

Retirement Is the Most Powerful Tax Tool You Have

While not traditionally thought of as a "write-off," retirement planning is one of the strongest tax strategies available to 1099 earners.

Solo 401(k) and SEP IRA plans allow consultants to shelter significant income while building long-term wealth. These contributions reduce taxable income legally and strategically.

High earners who neglect retirement planning often overpay taxes unnecessarily.

Avoiding the Most Common Tax Mistakes

Many consultants create problems by:

- Mixing personal and business expenses

- Failing to save for quarterly taxes

- Overstating deductions

- Ignoring recordkeeping

- Treating tax planning as an afterthought

Professionalism in safety should extend to finances. Clean books, clear separation of accounts, and proactive planning reduce stress and increase confidence.

Thinking Ahead: When Structure Matters

As income grows, so does the importance of structure.

At higher income levels, remaining a sole proprietor can become expensive. Transitioning to an LLC or S-Corp at the right time can reduce self-employment taxes and improve cash flow — but only when done intentionally.

This is not about rushing to restructure. It's about recognizing when complexity becomes beneficial rather than burdensome.

Operating Like an Owner Changes Everything

Consulting success is not just about technical skill — it's about stewardship.

When you understand where money goes, how taxes work, and how to protect what you earn, consulting becomes sustainable. Financial clarity creates freedom. Structure creates longevity.

A safety consultant who operates like a business owner doesn't just earn well — they keep what they earn.

And that is the difference between working independently and building something that lasts.

Chapter 11
Structuring Your Consulting Business — LLC vs. S-Corp and Mastering Quarterly Taxes

At a certain income level, how you structure your business matters as much as how much you earn.

Many safety consultants delay addressing business structure and tax planning because it feels complicated or intimidating. In reality, these two topics are the foundation of long-term financial efficiency. When done correctly, they reduce tax burden, improve cash flow, and eliminate year-end surprises.

This chapter is about clarity — understanding when structure matters and how to manage taxes proactively instead of reactively.

Why Structure Matters More as Income Grows

In the early stages of consulting, simplicity is often best. Operating as a sole proprietor or single-member LLC allows you to focus on building experience and clients without unnecessary complexity.

But as income increases, so does tax exposure.

At higher earnings, self-employment tax becomes a significant cost. Without intentional planning, consultants can lose tens of thousands of dollars annually simply because their structure hasn't evolved.

Structure is not about status. It's about efficiency.

Understanding the LLC Foundation

A single-member LLC is often the starting point for consultants. It provides legal separation between personal and business assets while maintaining simple tax treatment.

From a tax perspective, income flows directly to your personal return and is subject to:

- Federal income tax

- Self-employment tax

- State and local taxes

The LLC itself does not reduce taxes automatically — it provides legal protection and flexibility.

For many consultants, this structure works well until income reaches a level where self-employment taxes become excessive.

When an S-Corp Makes Sense

An S-Corporation is not a different business — it is a tax election.

When an LLC elects S-Corp status, income is split:

- Reasonable salary $\rightarrow$ subject to payroll taxes

- Owner distributions $\rightarrow$ not subject to self-employment tax

This split can create significant tax savings at higher income levels.

However, an S-Corp comes with added responsibility:

- Payroll processing

- Reasonable salary requirements

- Additional tax filings

- Increased accounting costs

Because of this, an S-Corp is not ideal for early-stage or inconsistent income.

Income Thresholds: When the Math Changes

While exact thresholds vary, many consultants begin seeing meaningful S-Corp benefits once net income consistently exceeds a certain range.

Below that level, the administrative burden often outweighs the tax savings.

Above it, the savings can be substantial.

This is not a decision to rush — it is a decision to make intentionally, with accurate numbers and professional guidance.

Reasonable Salary: The Most Misunderstood Rule

The IRS requires S-Corp owners to pay themselves a reasonable salary.

This salary must reflect:

- Your role

- Your experience

- Market rates

- Actual work performed

Underpaying salary to maximize distributions is one of the fastest ways to trigger scrutiny. Reasonable does not mean excessive — but it must be defensible.

A well-documented salary protects the tax advantage rather than jeopardizing it.

Quarterly Taxes: The Discipline That Saves You Stress

Regardless of structure, 1099 income requires quarterly tax payments.

These payments are not optional — they are estimates based on expected annual income. Failing to pay them leads to penalties, interest, and cash-flow surprises.

Quarterly payments force discipline. They prevent the common mistake of spending income that does not fully belong to you.

How to Calculate Quarterly Payments Correctly

Effective quarterly tax planning considers:

- Expected annual income

- Current deductions

- Retirement contributions

- Business structure

Rather than guessing, successful consultants work from projections. Adjustments are made throughout the year as income changes.

Paying slightly more than required is often safer than paying too little.

Cash Flow Strategy: Treat Taxes as a Fixed Expense

One of the smartest habits a consultant can develop is separating tax money immediately.

This can be done by:

- Automatically setting aside a percentage of income

- Using a separate tax savings account

- Treating tax payments as non-negotiable

This habit eliminates panic, preserves cash flow, and creates peace of mind.

How Structure and Quarterly Taxes Work Together

Business structure determines how much you owe.

Quarterly planning determines when and how you pay it.

When these two systems work together, taxes stop feeling chaotic. Income becomes predictable. Planning becomes easier.

This alignment is what allows consultants to grow confidently without fear of tax season.

Common Mistakes That Cost Real Money

Consultants often lose money by:

- Delaying structure changes too long

- Switching too early

- Ignoring payroll requirements

- Guessing quarterly payments

- Mixing business and personal finances

Every one of these mistakes is avoidable with planning.

Operating With Intention Changes Everything

The most successful consultants are not just skilled — they are organized.

They understand when structure matters, when simplicity is better, and how to stay ahead of taxes instead of reacting to them.

When your business is structured intentionally and taxes are planned proactively, consulting becomes sustainable, predictable, and scalable.

That's when independence stops feeling risky — and starts feeling powerful.

CHAPTER 12

SCALING WITHOUT LOSING CONTROL — GROWTH WITH INTENTION, NOT CHAOS

Growth is often portrayed as the ultimate goal in business. More clients. More revenue. More reach.

But in consulting — especially safety consulting — growth without control is one of the fastest ways to lose what you worked so hard to build.

The final stage of professional maturity is not expansion at all costs. It's intentional scaling — growing in a way that protects your standards, your reputation, and your life.

This chapter is about knowing when to grow, how to grow, and when not to.

Bigger Is Not Always Better

Many consultants assume scaling means hiring staff, taking on every project, and maximizing volume. In reality, that version of growth often replaces one form of burnout with another.

Uncontrolled growth creates:

- Quality issues

- Client dissatisfaction

- Legal exposure

- Exhaustion

- Loss of personal credibility

The most successful consultants understand that scale should increase leverage, not stress.

The First Question to Ask Before Scaling

Before expanding, ask yourself one honest question:

What problem am I trying to solve by growing?

If the answer is:

- "I'm overwhelmed"

- "I'm chasing revenue"

- "I feel pressure to grow"

Then the issue may not be scale — it may be boundaries, pricing, or client selection.

Scaling should solve a strategic problem, not avoid one.

Scaling Through Structure, Not Volume

True consulting scale rarely comes from more hours worked.

It comes from:

- Higher-value services

- Clear systems

- Repeatable processes

- Strong documentation

- Strategic partnerships

When systems are solid, workload becomes manageable. When systems are missing, even small growth feels chaotic.

Protecting Quality as You Grow

Your reputation is your business.

Every deliverable, recommendation, and interaction reflects your name — even when others assist you. Scaling without quality control damages trust faster than almost anything else.

If others support your work:

- Standards must be documented

- Expectations must be clear

- Final authority must remain yours

Growth should never dilute your professional identity.

The Right Way to Add Help

Adding support does not mean giving up control.

Many consultants scale successfully by:

- Outsourcing administrative tasks

- Using virtual assistants

- Partnering with trusted specialists

- Hiring project-based support

This allows you to stay focused on judgment, leadership, and client relationships — the highest-value parts of your role.

Choosing Clients Becomes More Important Than Finding Them

At scale, client selection matters more than marketing.

Not every opportunity deserves a yes. Some clients consume energy without returning value. Others push boundaries or create risk.

Experienced consultants learn to:

- Decline misaligned work

- Set firm scopes

- Walk away from poor-fit clients

Saying no is not a loss — it's a strategy.

Scaling Income Without Scaling Exposure

The most elegant growth models increase income while reducing risk.

This might include:

- Advisory retainers

- Program audits

- Training and mentorship

- Strategic planning support

- Thought leadership

These services rely on expertise rather than presence — allowing you to scale influence without scaling liability.

Control Is the Real Measure of Success

At the highest level, success is not revenue.

Success is:

- Control over your schedule

- Control over your clients

- Control over your standards

- Control over your energy

- Control over your future

When you maintain control, growth becomes sustainable. When control is lost, growth becomes a burden.

Knowing When to Stop Growing

The final skill of a seasoned consultant is knowing when enough is enough.

There is no requirement to build an empire. There is no obligation to expand endlessly. A well-run, highly respected consulting practice can be both profitable and contained.

Choosing stability over chaos is not a lack of ambition — it's wisdom.

The Full Circle of the Safety Career

This book began with a simple question:

Is safety the right career for you?

The answer, for those who make it to this chapter, is clear.

Safety can be more than a job.

More than a title.

More than a role.

It can be a career built on trust, independence, and integrity —
one that grows with you instead of consuming you.

When you scale intentionally, protect your standards, and stay
grounded in purpose, you don't just build a business.

You build a career that lasts.

ABOUT THE AUTHOR

Sharon Jost is a certified safety professional and founder of Vigilant Resources Consulting, bringing decades of field experience to the construction and industrial safety world. With credentials including CSP, CHST, ASP, and SHEP, she has earned her reputation through grit, expertise, and results — not shortcuts.

After building her career in environments where few women stood at the table, Sharon is passionate about helping others confidently break into the safety profession. Through mentorship, practical insight, and unfiltered honesty, she empowers readers to navigate certification paths, workplace dynamics, and leadership growth.

Breaking Into Safety is both a roadmap and a reality check — written by someone who has lived it.